MYSELF

I am away from my hometown and have a beautiful family. But I am unable to visit my hometown frequently. Now I am a little free nowadays and this is my time to meet my dreams. They came true with the help of my wife Vasundhara Devi as she left her dream for the family.

Thank you.

D. Suresh

INDEX

A BOOK OF TEN SHORT STORIES

Story-1:- A STORY OF SURPRISE

In the heart of a bustling city, where skyscrapers stretched towards the heavens and the streets buzzed with activity, there lived a young woman named Emma. Emma adored the holiday season with its twinkling lights, festive decorations, and the promise of joy and warmth.

As December approached, Emma found herself swept up in the whirlwind of holiday preparations.

Between her demanding job and busy social life, she barely had time to catch her breath. But amidst the chaos, there was one thing Emma looked forward to the most—a tradition she shared with her beloved grandmother, Rose.

Every year, on the first day of December, Emma and Rose would exchange handmade advent calendars filled with small surprises and treats. It was a tradition that brought them closer together, even though they lived miles apart.

This year, however, things were different. Rose had fallen ill and was unable to create her usual advent calendar for Emma. Heartbroken, Emma resolved to make her grandmother's favorite holiday tradition even more special.

She spent hours crafting a beautiful advent calendar, filling each tiny compartment with handwritten notes, cherished memories, and small trinkets that reminded her of their time together. With each passing day, Emma poured her love and affection into the calendar, hoping to bring a smile to her grandmother's face.

Meanwhile, Rose lay in her bed, her thoughts filled with worry and sadness. She longed to be with Emma, to share in the holiday cheer and create new memories together. But her failing health confined her to the four walls of her tiny apartment, far away from the bustling city where Emma lived.

One chilly December evening, as Emma returned home from work, she found a small package waiting for her on the doorstep. Curious, she tore it open to reveal a beautifully wrapped present and a handwritten note from her grandmother.

With trembling hands, Emma unwrapped the gift to reveal a delicate snow globe, its glass dome encasing a miniature winter scene complete with a quaint little village and a shimmering blanket of snow.

Tears welled up in Emma's eyes as she read her grandmother's note, in which Rose expressed her love and gratitude for their cherished tradition and the memories they had shared over the years.

Overwhelmed with emotion, Emma knew that this simple gift held more meaning than any extravagant present ever could. It was a symbol of their bond, a reminder that no matter the distance or the obstacles they faced, their love would always endure.

Filled with newfound determination, Emma rushed to her grandmother's side, snow globe in hand. As she embraced Rose in a warm hug, they both knew that this holiday season would be one they would never forget—a season of surprises, love, and the enduring magic of family.

Story-2: Frosty's Festive Adventure

In a quaint little village nestled amidst snow-capped mountains, there lived a mischievous snowman named Frosty. With his carrot nose, coal eyes, and twig arms, Frosty brought joy and laughter to the children who roamed the streets, his cheerful demeanor warming even the coldest of winter days.

As year end arrived and the village bustled with holiday preparations, Frosty felt a longing stirring within him. He had always dreamed of experiencing the magic of the holiday season firsthand—the twinkling lights, the scent of pine needles, and the warmth of a crackling fireplace.

Determined to make his dreams a reality, Frosty set out on a festive adventure unlike any other. With a gleeful twirl, he bounded through the village, his snowy footsteps leaving a trail of laughter and wonder in his wake.

First, Frosty decided to visit the village square, where the townsfolk were busy decorating a towering fir tree with twinkling lights and colorful ornaments. With a mischievous grin, he leaped into the air and landed on top of the tree, balancing precariously on the highest branch as the villagers gasped in surprise and delight.

Next, Frosty ventured into the nearby forest, where he stumbled upon a group of woodland creatures preparing for their own holiday festivities. With a twinkle in his eye, he joined in their merry dance, twirling and spinning beneath the starlit sky until the forest echoed with their laughter and song.

But Frosty's adventure was far from over. Determined to spread holiday cheer far and wide, he journeyed to the edge of the village, where he stumbled upon a lonely old cottage nestled amidst the snow-covered hills.

Peering through the frosted windowpane, Frosty spotted a solitary figure hunched over a table, his face etched with sorrow. Sensing the man's loneliness, Frosty pressed his coal eyes against the glass and gave a playful wink, his snowy smile lighting up the darkness like a beacon of hope.

Startled by the unexpected sight, the man stepped outside and gasped in astonishment as he beheld Frosty standing before him. With tears in his eyes, he thanked the cheerful snowman for bringing a ray of sunshine into his dreary world, promising to cherish the memory forever.

As the night grew darker and the stars began to twinkle overhead, Frosty knew that his festive adventure had come to an end. But as he trudged back towards the village, his heart brimming with joy and contentment, he realized that the true magic of the holiday season lay not in grand gestures or extravagant gifts, but in the simple act of spreading love and happiness wherever he went.

And so, with a merry twirl and a cheerful laugh, Frosty bid farewell to the village and disappeared into the snowy night, leaving behind a trail of footprints that sparkled like diamonds in the moonlight—a reminder that even the smallest snowflake can make a world of difference in the lives of those it touches.

---------/////-------

Story-3: The Miracle on Main Street

On Main Street, where the old brick buildings stood tall and the aroma of freshly baked pastries wafted through the air, there resided a community bound by tradition, friendship, and hope. But this year, as the holiday season approached, Main Street was shrouded in an unusual sense of gloom.

Businesses were struggling, and the festive spirit seemed to dim with each passing day. The twinkling lights that usually adorned the storefronts remained dark, and the usual laughter and chatter were replaced by murmurs of worry and uncertainty.

Amidst the somber atmosphere, a young girl named Lily refused to give up hope. With her bright eyes and cheerful smile, she was determined to bring joy back to Main Street and restore the magic of the holiday season.

Armed with nothing but her boundless optimism and a sprinkle of holiday magic, Lily embarked on a mission to spread cheer throughout the community. She started small, decorating the windows of her family's bakery with colorful paper snowflakes and twinkling lights, hoping to spark a glimmer of hope in the hearts of her neighbors.

But as the days passed and Main Street remained cloaked in darkness, Lily realized that more needed to be done. Drawing inspiration from an old story her grandmother had told her, Lily decided to organize a holiday festival unlike any other—a celebration of hope, kindness, and the power of community.

With the help of her friends and neighbors, Lily transformed Main Street into a winter wonderland, with festive decorations adorning every storefront and the sweet scent of cinnamon and sugar filling the air.

As the evening of the festival arrived, Main Street came alive with laughter and music, as families gathered to celebrate the magic of the season. There were carolers singing joyous melodies, children laughing as they twirled beneath the twinkling lights, and vendors selling steaming cups of hot cocoa and freshly baked cookies.

But the true miracle of Main Street occurred when a mysterious stranger arrived, bearing gifts for the entire community. With a twinkle in his eye and a smile on his lips, he handed out presents to young and old alike, spreading joy and laughter wherever he went.

As the night drew to a close and the last strains of music faded away, Main Street glowed with a warmth and light that had been absent for far too long. The once-dimmed lights now twinkled brightly, casting a magical glow over the cobblestone streets and filling the hearts of all who walked them with hope and joy.

And so, on that unforgettable night, the residents of Main Street discovered that miracles do exist—they're found in the kindness of strangers, the laughter of friends, and the unwavering belief in the magic of the holiday season.

As they bid farewell to the festive celebrations and returned to their homes, their hearts were lighter, their spirits lifted, and their faith in the power of love and community renewed once more. For on Main Street, where the old brick buildings stood tall and the aroma of freshly baked pastries lingered in the air, the true miracle of the season had been found—in the simple act of coming together and spreading joy to all who needed it most.

--------/////--------

Story-4: A Gift from the Heart

In a small Indian village nestled amidst lush green fields and rolling hills, there lived a young girl named Anaya. Anaya was known throughout the village for her kind heart and gentle spirit, always ready to lend a helping hand to those in need.

As the festival of Diwali approached, Anaya found herself filled with excitement. Diwali was a time of joy and celebration, a time when families came together to light oil lamps, exchange gifts, and share delicious sweets.

But this year, Anaya's family faced difficult times. Her father had fallen ill, and their meager savings were dwindling fast. Anaya longed to buy gifts for her family and friends, but she knew that they could not afford it.

Determined to make the festival special despite their hardships, Anaya set out to find a way to give her loved ones a gift from the heart. She spent hours collecting wildflowers from the fields, weaving them into colorful garlands to decorate their humble home.

Anaya's efforts did not go unnoticed. Her mother, seeing the love and dedication with which she worked, was filled with pride. "You are the true light of our family, Anaya," she said, her eyes shining with tears of gratitude.

Inspired by her daughter's selflessness, Anaya's mother decided to follow her example. She spent hours in the kitchen, preparing delicious sweets and savory snacks to share with their neighbors, spreading joy and happiness wherever she went.

As Diwali drew nearer, the village buzzed with excitement. The air was filled with the sound of laughter and music, and the streets were adorned with colorful decorations and twinkling lights.

On the morning of Diwali, Anaya woke up early, her heart full of anticipation. She helped her mother light oil lamps and arrange offerings at the family shrine, feeling a sense of peace and contentment wash over her.

But the true magic of Diwali came later that day, when Anaya's family gathered with their neighbors for a festive feast. As they sat together, sharing stories and laughter, Anaya presented each of them with a handmade garland, a symbol of her love and gratitude.

The villagers were touched by Anaya's gesture, and they in turn presented her with gifts of their own—simple tokens of appreciation, but given with love and sincerity.

As the day drew to a close and the stars twinkled overhead, Anaya realized that the greatest gift of all was the love and togetherness they shared as a community. In a world filled with darkness and uncertainty, their bond shone like a beacon of hope, illuminating the path forward with warmth and light.

And so, as Anaya drifted off to sleep that night, her heart was full of joy and gratitude. For she knew that no matter what challenges lay ahead, as long as they had each other, they would always find strength and solace in the love that bound them together—a gift from the heart that would never fade away.

--------/////--------

Story-5: Santa's Secret Workshop

In a quaint Indian village nestled amidst verdant fields and swaying palm trees, there lived a young boy named Arjun. Arjun had always been fascinated by the stories of Santa Claus and his magical workshop, where toys were crafted with love and care for children all around the world.

As the festive season approached, Arjun's excitement grew. He eagerly awaited the arrival of Santa Claus, hoping to catch a glimpse of the legendary figure and his workshop. But as the days passed and Christmas drew nearer, Arjun began to worry—his family, like many others in the village, could not afford to celebrate the holiday with lavish gifts and decorations.

Determined to bring some holiday cheer to his village, Arjun set out on a mission to create his own version of Santa's workshop. Armed with little more than his imagination and a few scraps of wood and cloth, he transformed his family's humble backyard into a bustling hub of creativity and joy.

With the help of his friends and neighbors, Arjun set to work crafting toys and decorations for the village children. They painted wooden dolls, stitched colorful quilts, and fashioned intricate ornaments from clay and beads, pouring their hearts and souls into each creation.

But as Christmas Eve approached, Arjun found himself facing a dilemma—how could they deliver the gifts to the children without them knowing? That's when he had an idea.

Gathering his friends together, Arjun revealed his plan for a secret nighttime mission. Under the cover of darkness, they would don disguises and sneak through the village, leaving gifts at the doorsteps of each home.

Excitement bubbled within them as they set out into the night, their hearts light with the anticipation of bringing joy to their community. As they tiptoed through the streets, they encountered other villagers doing the same, each one carrying a sack filled with gifts and treats.

Together, they moved like shadows, their laughter ringing out in the stillness of the night as they delivered their surprises to the children of the village. They watched from the shadows as sleepy-eyed youngsters emerged from their homes, their faces lighting up with wonder and delight at the sight of the unexpected gifts.

As dawn broke and the first light of Christmas morning painted the sky, Arjun and his friends returned home, their hearts full of joy and satisfaction. They knew that they had brought a little bit of magic to their village, and that was the greatest gift of all.

But the true magic of Christmas came later that day, when the villagers gathered in the village square for a festive celebration. Amidst the music and laughter, Arjun's mother stood up and thanked him for his selfless act of kindness, her eyes shining with pride.

And as they danced beneath the twinkling stars, Arjun realized that the spirit of Santa Claus was alive and well in their village—not in a faraway workshop at the North Pole, but in the hearts of each and every person who had come together to spread joy and love to those around them.

For in the end, it wasn't about the gifts or decorations—it was about the spirit of giving, of coming together as a community to share in the magic of the holiday season. And as they sang and danced beneath the starry sky, Arjun knew that this would be a Christmas to remember—a celebration of love, friendship, and the true meaning of the season.

---------////---------

Story-6: Wishes Upon a Star

In a serene Indian village nestled amidst lush green fields and swaying coconut palms, there lived a young girl named Kavya. Kavya was known throughout the village for her boundless optimism and her unwavering belief in the magic of the universe.

One clear night, as Kavya gazed up at the star-studded sky, she felt a flutter of excitement in her heart. It was said that on nights like these, when the stars shimmered brightly above, wishes made upon them had the power to come true.

With a smile on her lips and a glimmer of hope in her eyes, Kavya closed her eyes and made a wish. She wished for something that had been close to her heart for as long as she could remember—a better future for her village, where everyone lived in harmony and prosperity.

As she opened her eyes, she spotted a shooting star streaking across the sky, leaving behind a trail of sparkling light. Taking it as a sign, Kavya whispered her wish once more, her voice filled with determination and hope.

The next morning, Kavya awoke to find the village buzzing with excitement. Word had spread that a group of travelers was passing through, offering to grant the villagers' deepest wishes in exchange for a small favor.

Eager to see if her wish had come true, Kavya joined the crowd gathered in the village square. There, she found the travelers—a wise old sage and his companions, who listened attentively as the villagers shared their hopes and dreams.

When it was Kavya's turn, she took a deep breath and spoke from her heart. She told the travelers of her wish for a brighter future for her village, where everyone lived in harmony and prosperity, and where dreams had the chance to flourish like the stars in the sky.

The sage nodded solemnly, his eyes twinkling with understanding. He told Kavya and the villagers that wishes made with pure intentions and heartfelt sincerity had the power to move mountains and change destinies.

And so, with a wave of his hand and a few whispered words of ancient magic, the sage set about granting the villagers' wishes, one by one. He mended broken hearts, healed old wounds, and brought hope to those who had lost their way.

But when it came time for Kavya's wish to be granted, the sage paused. He explained to her that the power to change the future lay not in his hands, but in hers. He told her that her wish had already begun to come true, simply by believing in the possibility of a better tomorrow.

Filled with newfound determination, Kavya realized that she held the key to her village's destiny within her heart. She vowed to work tirelessly to make her wish a reality, to spread love and kindness wherever she went, and to inspire others to do the same.

And as she looked up at the sky that night, the stars twinkling brightly overhead, Kavya knew that no matter what challenges lay ahead, as long as she held onto her dreams and believed in the power of wishes made upon a star, anything was possible.

Story-7: Jingle Bells and Joy

In a bustling Indian city where the streets teemed with colorful markets and the air was filled with the sound of laughter and chatter, there lived a young woman named Priya. Priya was a spirited and adventurous soul, known for her infectious laughter and her love for her family.

Despite the hustle and bustle of city life, Priya's heart often longed for the quiet serenity of the English countryside, where her older brother, Rohan, lived with his family. Rohan had moved to England years ago to pursue his dreams, leaving behind fond memories of their childhood spent exploring the streets of their hometown.

As the holiday season approached, Priya found herself missing Rohan more than ever. It had been years since they had celebrated Christmas together, and the thought of spending the festive season apart filled her with a sense of longing and sadness.

Determined to reconnect with her brother and bring some holiday cheer into their lives, Priya hatched a plan. With a twinkle in her eye and a jingle in her step, she set out to surprise Rohan and his family with a visit to England for Christmas.

As she boarded the plane bound for London, Priya's heart raced with excitement. She couldn't wait to see the look of surprise on Rohan's face when she showed up on his doorstep, ready to celebrate the holidays together like they used to.

When Priya arrived in England, she was greeted by a blanket of snow that covered the countryside like a soft white quilt. The air was crisp and cold, filled with the scent of pine trees and the sound of jingle bells in the distance.

With a skip in her step, Priya made her way to Rohan's house, her heart pounding with anticipation. When she reached the familiar doorstep, she took a deep breath and rang the doorbell, her fingers tingling with excitement.

To her delight, Rohan answered the door with a puzzled expression, his eyes widening in surprise at the sight of his sister standing before him. Before he could utter a word, Priya enveloped him in a warm hug, her laughter echoing through the frosty air.

As Priya stepped inside the cozy warmth of Rohan's home, she was greeted by the joyful laughter of her niece and nephew, who rushed to greet her with open arms. The house was adorned with twinkling lights and colorful decorations, filling the air with the festive spirit of Christmas.

Together, Priya and her family spent the holiday season immersed in laughter and love. They decorated the Christmas tree, baked cookies, and sang carols by the fire, their hearts brimming with joy and gratitude for the precious moments they shared together.

As Christmas Day dawned, Priya looked around at her family gathered around the table, their faces aglow with happiness and love. In that moment, she realized that the true meaning of Christmas was not about presents or decorations, but about the gift of togetherness and the joy of being surrounded by the ones we love.

And as they raised their glasses in a toast to the holiday season, Priya knew that no matter where life may take them, the bond between her and her brother would always remain unbreakable—a testament to the enduring power of family and the magic of Christmas.

--------////--------

Story-8: Festive Adventure

In a lively Indian village nestled amidst the rolling hills and lush green fields, there lived a young boy named Raj. Raj was known throughout the village for his boundless energy and adventurous spirit, always eager to explore the world around him.

As the festive season approached, Raj felt a sense of excitement coursing through his veins. The village was abuzz with preparations for the upcoming celebrations, and Raj couldn't wait to embark on a festive adventure unlike any other.

With a twinkle in his eye and a spring in his step, Raj set out into the village, his heart filled with anticipation. As he wandered through the bustling marketplace, he marveled at the colorful decorations adorning the streets and the savory aromas wafting from the food stalls.

But Raj's festive adventure truly began when he stumbled upon a group of musicians playing joyful melodies beneath the shade of a banyan tree. Drawn by the lively beat of the drums and the melodious strains of the flute, Raj joined in the dance, twirling and spinning with abandon as the music filled the air with merriment.

As the sun dipped below the horizon and the sky was painted in hues of pink and orange, Raj found himself drawn to the village temple, where the air was thick with the scent of incense and the sound of bells echoed through the night.

Inside, he discovered a group of villagers gathered in prayer, their faces aglow with devotion and reverence. Inspired by their faith, Raj joined them in offering prayers of gratitude for the blessings of the past year and wishes for prosperity in the year to come.

But Raj's festive adventure was far from over. With the night still young and his spirit soaring, he ventured into the surrounding countryside, where he stumbled upon a group of children gathered around a bonfire, their faces illuminated by its warm glow.

Intrigued, Raj approached them and discovered that they were telling stories of ancient legends and folklore passed down through generations. With rapt attention, he listened as they recounted tales of gods and goddesses, heroes and villains, their words weaving a tapestry of magic and wonder.

As the fire crackled and the stars twinkled overhead, Raj felt a sense of belonging wash over him. Here, surrounded by friends old and new, he realized that the true spirit of the festive season lay not in grand gestures or extravagant celebrations, but in the simple joys of togetherness and community.

And as he bid farewell to his newfound friends and made his way back to the village, Raj knew that he would carry the memories of his festive adventure in his heart forever. For on this magical night, he had discovered that the true meaning of the festive season was not just about celebrating traditions or rituals, but about embracing the spirit of joy, love, and unity that bound them all together as a community.

Story-9: Mind of Evergreen

In the heart of a dense forest, where sunlight filtered through the thick canopy of evergreen trees and the air was filled with the earthy scent of moss and pine, there stood a majestic old tree known as the Evergreen. It was said that the Evergreen possessed a wisdom beyond its years, its roots deeply intertwined with the secrets of the forest.

For centuries, the Evergreen had stood sentinel over the forest, watching as seasons changed and generations passed. Its branches stretched towards the sky, reaching for the sun, while its roots delved deep into the earth, drawing sustenance and strength from the soil.

But beneath its silent exterior lay a mind as vast and ancient as the forest itself—a mind filled with memories of ages past and visions of the future yet to come.

One crisp autumn morning, as the leaves began to turn golden and the forest echoed with the sound of rustling leaves, a young girl named Maya stumbled upon the Evergreen while exploring the woods near her home. Intrigued by its towering presence and the air of mystery that surrounded it, Maya approached the tree with wonder in her eyes.

To her surprise, as Maya reached out to touch the rough bark of the Evergreen, she felt a strange sensation wash over her—a sensation that seemed to whisper of forgotten dreams and untold stories hidden within the depths of the forest.

In that moment, Maya felt a connection unlike any she had ever known. It was as if the Evergreen was reaching out to her, inviting her to share in its ancient wisdom and timeless secrets.

With a sense of awe and reverence, Maya closed her eyes and allowed herself to be swept away by the whispers of the Evergreen. She felt herself drifting through time and space, her mind entwined with the mind of the tree, as they journeyed together through the memories of ages past.

She saw the forest as it once was, teeming with life and vibrant energy, its inhabitants living in harmony with the rhythms of nature. She witnessed the changing seasons, from the bursting forth of new life in spring to the quiet introspection of winter's embrace.

But Maya also saw the scars that marred the landscape—the scars left by human hands, careless and destructive in their quest for power and dominion over the land. She saw the trees felled and the rivers polluted, the once-thriving ecosystem brought to the brink of collapse by greed and ignorance.

As the vision faded and Maya opened her eyes, she found herself standing once more before the Evergreen, her heart heavy with the weight of what she had seen. But amidst the sorrow, there was also a glimmer of hope—a hope born from the realization that it was not too late to change the course of destiny, to heal the wounds of the earth and restore balance to the forest.

With newfound determination, Maya vowed to honor the wisdom of the Evergreen and protect the natural world for generations to come. She knew that the mind of the Evergreen would always be there to guide her, its roots entwined with hers, as together they embarked on a journey to safeguard the future of the forest and all who called it home.

——----<<>>-----

Story-10

A Beachside Holiday with Max

The sun dipped low over the horizon, casting a golden glow upon the tranquil beach. A gentle breeze carried the salty scent of the ocean, while the rhythmic sound of waves lapping against the shore provided a soothing melody. It was the perfect setting for a holiday retreat, and Sarah couldn't have been happier to escape the hustle and bustle of city life for a few days of relaxation.

Nestled amidst the dunes stood a quaint beach house, its weathered wooden exterior blending seamlessly with the natural surroundings. Inside, cozy furnishings invited guests to unwind and enjoy the simple pleasures of coastal living. Sarah had been looking forward to this getaway for weeks, and she couldn't wait to share the experience with her faithful companion, Max.

Max, her loyal golden retriever, bounded eagerly beside her as they approached the beach house. His tail wagged furiously, and his eyes sparkled with excitement at the prospect of exploring their new surroundings. Sarah chuckled at his enthusiasm, feeling grateful for his unwavering companionship.

Once inside, Sarah set about making the beach house feel like home. She opened the windows to let in the salty breeze, adorned the living room with seashell decorations, and laid out a cozy blanket for Max near the fireplace. With everything in place, she couldn't resist slipping into her swimsuit and heading down to the beach for a leisurely stroll.

Max raced ahead, his sandy fur catching the sunlight as he bounded across the shore. Sarah followed at a more leisurely pace, relishing the feel of warm sand between her toes and the gentle caress of the ocean breeze against her skin. She breathed in deeply, allowing the serenity of the moment to wash over her.

As the day faded into evening, Sarah and Max returned to the beach house, tired but content. They dined al fresco on the deck, savoring the flavors of freshly grilled seafood as they watched the sun set over the horizon. The sky blazed with hues of orange and pink, casting a mesmerizing glow over the landscape.

With the stars twinkling overhead, Sarah and Max curled up by the fireplace, lost in the comforting embrace of each other's company. Max's gentle snores filled the room, a testament to the day's adventures and the contentment of a dog who was truly at home.

In the days that followed, Sarah and Max made the most of their time at the beach house. They explored hidden coves and secret tide pools, played fetch along the shoreline, and basked in the warmth of the sun. Each moment was a cherished memory, a testament to the bond between a girl and her dog.

As their holiday drew to a close, Sarah found herself reluctant to leave the tranquility of the beach house behind. But as she packed their belongings and prepared to depart, she knew that she would carry the memories of their time together in her heart forever.

With one last glance back at the beach house, Sarah smiled, knowing that she and Max would return again someday to create new memories by the sea. For now, they would carry the spirit of their beachside holiday with them wherever they went, a reminder of the simple joys that awaited them just

beyond the horizon.

-------////-------